The Elder Widow's Walk
A Personal Inner Journey and Guide for Bereaved Widows 65 and Beyond

Lucille Ann Meltz

Praise for The Elder Widow's Walk

"If you are a newly bereaved woman and your question is "how am I going to go on?", this is the book to read; truthful openhearted, and practical."
~ *Kristine Watson, LCPC, Grief Counselor.*

~~~~~

Reading Lucille's book is like being with a dear and wise friend who has traveled this lonely, painful path and can hold the space for us to feel our grief knowing we are not crazy. When we have been blessed with a deep love, the grief is like nothing we have ever known. Lucille has a capacity to share her experience in a way that empowers the reader. With wisdom realized from her deep encounter with her own grief and loss, her brilliant honesty, and her generous sharing of practices that helped her, we discover grief as a passage to birthing a new self. I heartily recommend this book to anyone struggling with the darkness of grief. It offers hope, comfort and the real possibility of a life lived with even deeper love.

~ *Arline Saturdayborn, teacher, Mindfulness and Compassion*

~~~~~

This precious, raw and hopeful book offers a window into the heart, mind and body of an older woman who has survived her Beloved husband. Grief is a demanding, experiential assault to body, mind, and heart. Meltz writes honestly about the many ways she no longer belongs to herself in the familiar ways after her husband's death. She is an elder widow and ageing is an integral part of her grieving process. She also interweaves appalling statistics and research findings that speak to the isolation and financial challenges that "women widows of a certain age" face.

Toward the end of her two-year grief immersion, Meltz writes about how she grew beyond grief to embrace her future. As a result of her own immersion in grief, she offers ideas and tools that empowered her to begin to reclaim her life.

This small book is a heart touchstone for elder women widows. It is also a look inside for family and friends who wish to support elder widows through grief and welcome them to their new life, when the time is right.

~ *Rosalie Deer Heart, author of Healing Grief — A Mother's Story and Living Future Pull*

The Elder Widow's Walk

A Personal Inner Journey and Guide for Bereaved Widows 65 and Beyond

Lucille Ann Meltz

FOR MARTY,
THE COMPANION OF MY HEART,
FOR ALL YOU WERE AND CONTINUE TO BE TO
ME.
BECAUSE LIFE IS TO BE LIVED
AND LOVE NEVER DIES.

PREFACE
March 18, 2015, 4:10 AM

The hospice cot is lumpy and uncomfortable. I am restless and exhausted. Just as it seems sleep might come, I hear it. My husband's rasping, gasping breath. Deep breaths that come erratically and then vanish along with his long-term struggle for life.

I jolt out of bed, rush to his bedside a few feet away and ring for the nurse. Holding his hand I am aware that he looks so peaceful, quiet and rested, as if he will soon awake refreshed, smile at me and say my name. I know it is the end and yet my need for him has not diminished and still feeds my delusion.

The kindly nurse arrives, takes his pulse and tells me, yes, it is only a matter of minutes now. I lie down next to him, holding his lightened, wasted body in my arms, and weeping softly repeat: "Marty, oh Marty, it's alright. It's over. The pain is over. I am here. No more suffering. I love you, I am with you. I love you…"

One last breath. I feel the stillness in his body. My beloved husband of 47 years is gone.

Two months earlier I had turned seventy. And now I belonged to an all too numerous population of women: elder widows. My husband's prolonged passage of deep suffering and misery was over. Mine had barely begun.

As I write this, 18 months later, the intense journey of profound loss, extreme isolation, interminable fears and anxieties, heartbreak and soul-searching continues, although its ebbs and tides weaken. What comes now, little by little, more and more, are the gentle promises and beginnings of growth, renewal and fresh life perspectives.

It is not, however, only the essence of my elder widow's story that I offer to all my sisters, all the widows of advancing years who know their lives are forever transformed and yet still changing, who intuitively understand that their loss is unique because of their age, but who feel lost and alone in a world that devalues the pain of that loss *because* of their age. To all the elder widows who resonate with my journey, I also offer acknowledgement of what you have endured and continue to endure. I offer compassion for your extraordinary struggles too often forgotten by those around you. And I invite you to consider some of the spiritual and emotional practices that have kept me from plunging into total breakdown.

To all widows 65 and beyond still held in the grips of life's most heart-stabbing experience, I write this to affirm that you too can survive, and to help you find, through your own unparalleled loss, the exceptional gift of spiritual strength, inner power and the true uplifting wisdom of the elder widow.

CHAPTER ONE
AN ELDER WIDOW'S REALITY CHALLENGE

If you are a widow age 65 or more, you are not alone. But it certainly may feel as if you are.

In the United States, *almost half of all women over 65 are widows — more than eleven million women.* There are five times as many widows as widowers among the elderly. If any other social or personal tragedy involved or affected such a phenomenal number of people, surely there would be mega-media coverage, extensive support networks, widespread government grants and programs and promotion of universal awareness of the complicated issues involved.

However, since becoming a widow at age 70, despite having earnestly sought to find understanding and support in the greater world beyond family and friends, I have only uncovered a few sparse articles, blogs and selected parts of books on aging that addressed at all the unique concerns of the elder widow.

The elder widow's life is a reality that only others who share that experience can completely understand. It is a reality, therefore, colored by alienation and, too often, severe debilitating loneliness.

When my husband died I was living temporarily in another state, over 1700 miles from home. I had moved there to be closer to family after transferring my husband from one long-term care facility here in Maine to one in North Carolina, nearer to our daughter and son-in-law. His death brought an immediate loving response from close family and friends who showered me for a brief time with love and caring attention. Yet, as is the norm following any death, people return to their own lives. I was living in rented short-term housing in a town where I knew no one, and after everyone left and the calls subsided, I was the most alone that I have ever felt in my life. I could not reach out to make new connections where I was, as I felt incapable of even talking to anyone who did not know Marty. I was aware that sharing too much with my daughter was an excessive burden on her, an only child dealing with her own grief.

I am blessed with many kind, loving and empathetic friends scattered over six or seven states. They called to check on me, cried on the phone with me, and one dear friend even traveled from Maine to be with me for two weeks. But with the pain of my loss so raw and unbridled, with the future looking so frightening to a woman alone at my age, and being so far from any consistent support base, it was impossible to feel much sustained comfort or anything more than incredible aloneness.

Even when I returned to Maine, two months after his death, I felt that I no longer truly belonged to the network of women with whom I often shared "husband tales." When friends invited me to join them with their husbands I felt odd, not part of their lifestyles any longer. I did not fit into any grouping of couples. Nor did I feel I could saddle my friends with the continued, seemingly endless pain of my grief. I know all my family and friends care about me. I also know my life now is forever different.

After 47 years of being with my heart's closest companion, there is a reality of bottomless loneliness that can never truly be described to anyone who does not experience it.

According to "widowhood.org," 75 percent of an elder widow's support base is lost following the death of her spouse.

Any widow, regardless of age, feels isolated, cut-off from other coupled friends, alienated by new, often overwhelming post-death responsibilities and painfully lost without the major support of her live-in companion. But for the elder widow there is oftentimes the additional reality of already being cut off in many ways from support networks.

A number of elderly women no longer drive at night, curtailing their ability to gather with others in groups or social functions. The health issues of aging can limit mobility and cognition while also affecting a widow's desire to engage in social activities. *A full sixty percent of all elder widows come down with a serious illness within 6 to 12 months following their husband's death,* making it even more difficult to deal with their grief or be connected to community, friends and family.

I believe the staggering stress of losing one's long term life partner may create an immune suppressing effect. Before my husband's passing, even with the enormous stress of his continued physical decline over three years, I had not even had a cold in over five years. I was healthy and physically fit, always consistent with my exercise and healthy diet. But two weeks after his death I became ill with a respiratory infection that I could not shake, lasting almost 4 months. Many elder women already have compromised immune systems and are unable to fight off new assaults on their physical body.

There is perhaps, as well, the fear that married women may have of being drawn too closely into the well of sorrow that a new widow may exhibit. Having lived in retirement communities I have found that denial about one's own death or one's spouse's death can create an additional isolation factor around an elderly widow. There seems to be an irrational fear that contact with someone who has had death around them will draw death to you. Or the even more unsubstantiated fear that an elder widow is looking to find a new mate, and older married men are the assumed target since there are so few unmarried men around of advancing age.

When I was growing up, over 50 years ago, as the third generation of an Italian-American family, I lived with my parents and maternal grandparents as well as an elderly great uncle. It was the norm in my childhood neighborhood for older widows to be sharing a home with their adult children and grandchildren. So when an aging parent died there was always family immediately available to help support the remaining parent, who was usually a woman. There was also an entire neighborhood of older widows around with whom to easily share talks, sorrows, recipes and grandchildren stories. Today multi-generational households are statistically rare. Elderly widows live alone much more now than 40 years ago when only 44 percent of all widows over 65 lived alone. *Today 70 percent of all elderly widows live alone, often thousands of miles away from any close family support.*

Elder widows are also commonly plagued by financial issues that increase their isolation and despair. *Sixty percent of all the poor elderly are widows.* For the past 30 years or more, the rate of poverty among elderly widows has been 3 to 4 times higher than it is among elderly married women. An elderly widow loses an average of 40% of her social security income and often any pension or health care benefits that were covered by her husband's income. So while suddenly having to take over many responsibilities that may have been managed by her husband such as household repairs, car maintenance or financial management, an elder widow may now be dealing with considerably less financial resources to handle her new roles. Limited income also curtails choices like health care options, living arrangements, possibilities of diversion and social connection and support through travel or outings with groups or tours. All of this further complicates her sense of alienation and feeling that there is no way out.

An elder widow today is more likely to have had less life experience in running a household alone or developing the mental and emotional resources to live by herself. Over half of women married in the 1960s and 70s stayed married to the same man for 30 years or more. And women in those years tended to marry younger than today, generally in their early twenties. *This means that today's elder widow is most likely a woman whose life experience involved little time, if any, living alone before becoming coupled.* The death of a spouse becomes, then, not only a shock in losing one's life partner, but also in figuring out, at an older, less adaptive age, how to manage the simple daily tasks of living all alone.

When one loses a husband in younger years, there is often work to distract and engage a widow's attention and time as well as afford opportunities for community and additional income. At 65 and beyond, despite the new trend for elders to work longer, less than 15% of women over 65 are still in the work force. Most elder widows have been out of the work place for some time or have created work that keeps them at home. This is not a time of life when a career ladder is present, and no easy income opportunities appear beyond minimum wage. An elder widow too often has to worry about economic survival, needing to salvage any funds available for the very near onset of old age and the host of possible medical costs. At 45 a widow can look to investing any financial resources or disposable income to grow for the long term. At 65 or more, the long term is no longer an option.

In our Internet-based society many find solace, connection or diversion during times of great distress in social media, e-mail conversations and computer-based stimulation. But for some elders, especially those living in very isolated areas or restricted by finances, the Internet is a limited resource, providing an experience that seems complicated, out of reach or stressful in itself. This becomes then an additional source of feeling cut off, discounted and generally obsolete. An elder widow may likely be seeking the old fashioned comfort of close family, but is then daily being reminded by the greater culture that the way to experience connection is something that may make her feel more alienated.

The death of a spouse at any age is the number one stressor on the Holmes-Rahe Stress Inventory, a stress scale used by therapists, physicians and mental health workers to measure the degree of stress a person is currently experiencing in life and to predict the likelihood of serious illness as a result of that stress. This means that the loss of one's life partner is one of life's most devastating events and creates more internal anxiety, grief, heartache and numbing psycho-spiritual pain than any other of life's losses.

This stress measurement, however, does not take into account the reality of the elder widow whose loss may be further compounded by her stage of life and gender, and by a legion of additional physical, economic, emotional and societal challenges. I believe that *for women 65 and older who have lost their husbands, the stress level can be off the scale.* There is yet no true societal acknowledgement of what an elder widow's journey frequently entails.

Of course, there are elder widows who have strong financial resources, close knit and geographically available family and community, superb health and fulfilling work, and these widows have a clearer path toward self-renewal. However, it seems that to become an elder widow frequently means to create your own way. It means a time of finding solace and comfort from within. A time of facing the greatest transition life deals you and coming to terms with a life dramatically and essentially changed while confronting the challenges of your age.

This is the elder widow's walk that I know and now address for others.

If this is your walk, I believe, through my own journey, that with resilience, courage, emotional awareness, inner strength and faith, the new reality that can emerge will bring you a sense of freedom and renewal. You can survive this journey. You can thrive again.

And I am walking beside you.

CHAPTER TWO
FIRST, YOU GRIEVE ...

And then you grieve again and again and again.

As a master's degree level personal life coach and former school guidance counselor and independent consultant, I have taught many classes and workshops on the process of grief. I have coached numerous others individually about dealing with their own grief. When my husband first had open heart surgery or when he became ill with a life threatening infection and again when he had two mega strokes and yet again when he had 2 critical bouts with pneumonia...I clearly knew that he could die. There were a number of desperate ER trips and then middle-of-the-night phone calls when he was in nursing care or in the hospital, all times when I actually thought he was dying. I believed I was prepared, with my professional experience and through the experience of 2 1/2 years of his ongoing decline, for the worst.

I was so wrong.

Marty died in the calming peace and supportive environment of hospice. He died what could be called "a good death" surrounded by loving family and according to his wishes. But his death still completely undid me. I seemed totally unable to accept the reality of his passing. I was numb, shocked and in deep depression for many, many months. I planned and organized his memorial, saw to the tasks of daily life, many of which, like car maintenance, I had never undertaken alone, and yet I could not find my own center, my own sense of self. I felt more lost and disoriented than I have ever felt in my life. Tears and crying overtook me numerous times daily in ways I could never have imagined, at the most inappropriate times and in the most unexpected places.

Almost two years later I still cry every day, though not as intensely or as long. I still expect to see him come in the door or hear his voice from another room, but now I am more often comforted than distressed by that illusion. I miss his caress and hugs and touch every night and wake up each day to the sad reminder that he is not next to me.

Then I talk to him, pray for him and call his name
as I move into my daily living.

Grief does not just end.

There is no true closure, even as one
moves into greater acceptance. There are
changes and stages and none of it is
predictable, and every widow grieves in her
own time and in her own way.

Yet for the elder widow it is a process
deeply intensified by her time of life.

Anyone who has studied the dynamics of
grieving knows that grief is cumulative. Any
loss you experience has the innate and strong
potential for dredging up old losses,
especially those that have not been fully
released or processed. Life is full of large and
small losses and it is not always possible to
fully acknowledge the ache of those losses.
And when you don't own the grief, each loss
becomes a part of your psyche, incorporated
into the latest opportunity to feel sorrow
when a fresh loss occurs.

When you lose a loved one at 40, you may also be feeling the pain of losing your pet dog at 10, a close friend who moved away at 20, a childhood home that no longer exists, a missed opportunity for the dream job at 30...a host of previous losses that you may or may not even be conscious of grieving.

At 65 and beyond as an elder widow, you have already experienced a long lifetime of endless possible losses: loss of parents, friends, homes, animal companions, children leaving home, youthfulness, work identity, mobility, physical vitality, personal power, status, financial security, siblings, extended family members and community acquaintances. As a woman, you have also probably had to acknowledge a certain sense of loss of physical sexual attractiveness defined by our youth oriented society, which means becoming more and more invisible in the greater culture.

As an elder widow you are likely plagued by more losses than you may even be able to enumerate, yet they exist in a level of your consciousness and make your latest bereavement, the heartache of losing your life's partner, the number one stressor on the Stress Scale, far deeper, more severe, and much more powerful.

You are not imagining how difficult it is.
It is that difficult and more.
And I know it can be overwhelming.

Yet what I have learned, and am still learning, is that grief transforms itself and in the process transforms us. We pass through its fire to become reborn.

There is never true closure. Closure is a myth. *But there is change and movement and opening to greater acceptance.*

Even after decades of psycho-spiritual work on myself and with others, the grief over the loss of my beloved husband has brought me to my knees. And in that process of surrender to the agonizing pain and absolute submission to its power, I have been able to allow the greatest depth of feeling to emerge. Depression has become my ally through allowing me to truly feel the pain. And release of sorrow has opened an inner space for my intuition to guide me daily into a greater stage of grace.

Grief is a complicated and non-linear process. We have known now for over 40 years, since the pioneering death-and-dying work of Elizabeth Kubler-Ross, that the five major stages of loss may come and go at different times and at differing levels of intensity. And it is widely recognized that we each experience grief in individual and unique ways. You may find people telling you that you are in "shock" or "denial" or "depression" or "anger." However, what anyone tells you is his or her own experience of you in that moment. And what anyone has researched is only a summary of many people's experiences. *What truly matters is understanding your own process.* What is your life situation telling you, what are your own feelings about and how do you allow grief to lead you out of the pit of darkness toward the greater light?

As an elder woman dealing with the myriad issues of being widowed at an advanced age, I found that the first order of business was to give myself over to my profound grief. To allow myself to feel it all and know *that* was exactly what I needed. Grieving and appreciating the process of grief became the agonizing but necessary gateway to opening to a life that again includes more meaning, connection, fresh wisdom and renewal.

Understanding the commonality of the stages of loss and what you are emotionally experiencing can help you cope with loss a bit easier as you realize that what you are feeling is completely normal and appropriate. And now, as an elder widow revisiting the countless losses of your life and beginning the long journey of coming to terms with the loss of your spouse, this is a time not only of recognizing the underlying role of previous losses, but of self-forgiveness for any role you played in those losses that still pains you. It's a time to permit yourself the time and space to know, at a deep level, that being an elder widow rewrites, in new ways, the definition and stages of grief and loss.

~~~~~

When my friend from Maine came to visit me in North Carolina a few weeks after Marty died, my daughter and I drove together to pick her up at the airport. As we arrived at the terminal and parked the car, I found myself suddenly feeling very excited, anticipating something good, joyful and positive – feelings definitely out of sync with my ever-present grief. What I suddenly realized in that moment was that although I had been talking about looking forward to seeing my friend Heidi, the belief I really held was that I was expecting Marty to arrive, as he had many times before at airports in our life together. I had hoped, in my own grief-stricken world, that he had simply been away for awhile and was now returning to me. When I recognized the true reality, all my positive feelings evaporated.

DENIAL/SHOCK: This is often the first stage of grief as you struggle to survive the surreal feeling that your beloved husband is truly gone. It may feel like he is only temporarily missing and will return shortly. A sense of overall numbness, mental and emotional fogginess, and a sense of non-belief (like seeing him in a crowd or thinking the phone ringing is him calling) take over. This is all actually a cushion to the heart-pounding terror of knowing that your world is now shattered. Denial helps you pace your grief and permits you to handle, in smaller steps, the reality of your enormous loss. Denial can be a stage of comforting grace. It keeps you blind at a time when you are not yet ready to see.

Denial and shock can go in and out, like all the stages of grief. Almost two years later I still often experience times when I am busy doing something and all of a sudden I am hit with the thought, *Oh my God, Marty is gone, it cannot be.* The distracting business of being involved in a project, a book, an event, an outing, all can serve to keep us more whole and yet also can serve to keep the truth at bay. There is nothing wrong or negative about being in denial unless, like any stage, we find we are living there all the time. The value of awareness of any stage is knowing and understanding where you are and asking yourself: how does it serve you in the moment and where does it lead you?

ANGER: When denial is not in force and you are living with the seemingly endless heartache of your now solitary life, you may find yourself angry much more than normal. You may feel outrage at doctors, caregivers, someone who may have been or should have been held responsible for your husband's death (as in an auto accident). Unprovoked, you are furious at family, at friends, even at your husband or at God. You feel abandoned, mad, and life seems completely unfair. Your anger can be triggered by simply meeting another man your husband's age or by being with a friend who talks about her living, healthy husband. It may not make much sense, but anger is a powerful emotion telling you to delve into your pain and fears. It is a reminder of how deeply you loved him. And it can be an opening to move more gently into the release of your grief.

As an elder widow the aspect of dealing with all the humdrum world, suddenly as a single woman after almost 50 years with a life partner, made me angry a good bit of the time. Anger is not a feeling I am easily prone to, but suddenly it seemed so unfair to me that I was left behind, unprepared, to deal alone with all the myriad financial matters, bank records, income tax, credit cards, medical bills, insurance issues, car maintenance, house repairs – so many areas of life that my husband had more than willingly managed – and managed well for our entire life together. I wanted to scream every time I heard a customer representative tell me "I am sorry for your loss." It felt hollow and shallow and my pain was so much greater than mere words could reach.

Anger, then, was all I had. And it taught me that I needed to go deeper into my pain and find the place where my anger was born.

What I have realized through my anger is that guilt was holding me hostage to anger. I recognized the guilt I felt over all I believe I "should have done" to keep my husband alive, to make him healthy.

GUILT/BARGAINING: "What if..?" "If only ..." These are the repetitive self-statements you may lose yourself in. You ache for the impossible opportunity to rewrite the past, go back in time and find the cause of the illness, avoid the fatal accident or be there for your husband in ways you could not be. Guilt is the companion to this type of unreal bargaining as you find fault in whatever you think you could have or should have done to keep your husband with you. You may even feel guilty for simply being alive when he is not. Returning to the past and re-making your history is the illusion which temporarily alleviates the intensity of loss and helps you, with time, to adjust to your new reality.

More than a year after Marty died, while I was driving on one of the local back country roads, a beautiful doe came rapidly out of the woods and ran right into the left side of my car by the driver's door. I did not see her until her sweet face was right up at my driver's side window. She hit the car hard enough to push it to the side of the road and then took off, leaving me in a stunned state. I became almost hysterical even though I was not hurt, for all I could think of was the poor doe, fearing she was injured, and had run off into the woods alone to suffer and die. I sat alone in my car, crying out to the deer amidst my tears, "Oh I am so sorry, I am so sorry."

Soon a young couple came by and stopped to see if I was alright. The young man, an experienced hunter, examined the damage to my car, noticing that there was no sign of blood or tissue left on the car. Although the deer was probably bruised and shocked, it would recover. He also told me that there was no way the accident was my fault. The deer had run into me.

My sense of guilt, however, did not diminish. I cried much of that day for the deer, but soon realized that the accident with the deer was really about my experience with Marty. For despite so many friends and family members telling me what a devoted, loving and strong advocate and wife I was to Marty during his seemingly endless struggle, I was still often plagued after his death with the sense that there was something more I should have done: found another doctor, insisted that he undergo a certain surgery or been more present with him during his nine-month stay in nursing homes. Even though I did not cause his illnesses and strokes, just thinking about his constant torturous misery could still bring deep pain and guilt. I recall his dependency on me to sort it all out, to be there for him when he could no longer speak or walk or care much for himself. The responsibility I felt was so overpowering that I felt I could not forgive myself if he did not survive or become healthy again. And of course, he did not thrive or survive. So the part of me that returns to the past and all its horror blames me, telling me I am the one who failed him. When that happens I am coming to recognize that what I am doing is escaping the possibility of claiming my own life. Of becoming a woman in her elder years who has survived the very worst and can continue to live.

Yet I also know that my guilt and need to relive the past, like denial, keep reality hidden gracefully. For whenever I fall into those places, I unwittingly give myself permission to live the illusion that I can recreate all the history of his physical decline and create a new ending. It is the pause I desperately need in the moment before I am fully ready to accept what lies ahead and to forgive myself for the reality of simply having been an imperfect human being.

DEPRESSION: Anger or guilt is often followed by or interspersed with depression as your attention moves more fully to the recognition of the present and the knowing that your dearest love will never return. Your sadness feels more extreme than you could ever have imagined, even if you felt that you were prepared for his passing. Sadness overwhelms you and you wonder, "What's the point of going on?" You feel lethargic with little or no energy or motivation. You feel withdrawn and alone and alienated. *Nothing seems to matter anymore.* Depression is the ultimate sense of sorrow and yet a normal and appropriate response to the loss of your life's dearest companion.

In the early months after Marty's death, I slept longer nights and took frequent naps because being awake meant having to face pain which was much too intense. And when I was awake I broke into crying spells just seeing his photo or being in a place we frequented together, even so ordinary a place as our supermarket. It was difficult for me to make decisions, something that had never been a problem for me before. Sometimes I felt there was no purpose to my life any longer. I had given up the majority of my independent work to be his caregiver and no longer felt any inspiration to return to most of it. I often forced myself just to get up each day and take decent physical care of myself only for the sake of my daughter, whom I could not bear to leave an adult orphan.

I still mourn him every day and experience anew the heartbreak for all he endured, and I weep for all the unique love, closeness and support that is forever gone. The crying may be considerably less frequent and lengthy, but it is no less real.

Yet I acknowledge that, for me, the times of depression have been a godsend. They have allowed me to release years of unaddressed grief, sadness and loss I did not allow myself to feel during the time my husband was in constant physical crisis, pain and emotional turmoil. I know now that the days and nights of lonely weeping were essential medicine for my soul that are bringing me closer to feeling whole again, even though never again the woman I used to be.

Depression can be set off at unexpected times and yet also be predictable. Holidays, anniversaries and birthdays are all occasions when the absence of your loved one is so obvious and overwhelming that you feel, even years after his passing, that you are still grieving. Just when you think perhaps you are moving forward in your life, you are reminded, cruelly it seems, by the culture around you of your loss. Couples your age enjoying a holiday in a restaurant, or advertisements for family get-togethers over Thanksgiving dinner, may make you wish you could just withdraw from the world or hide under the covers.

Like all phases of grief, depression comes and goes. We move 3 steps forward and 2 back. This, as hard as it sounds, is the normal process of shedding the immobilizing heartache that keeps us from accepting what is: a new life phase.

ACCEPTANCE: Acceptance does *not* mean being "OK" with what you have lost: your life's partner and your entire way of life. Acceptance means recognizing that your loss is the new reality for you and you are coming to terms with how to live with it. It means, little by little, accepting that your life is forever changed, that you cannot return to what it was before his death. You have new roles, new responsibilities and new anxieties and fears to cope with. You now seek help for those responsibilities or create new directions and new relationships in your life to support you. More and more you accept all the feelings you still have about losing your spouse, but they no longer rule your daily life. You honor more of your own needs. *This is by no means a sudden or separate stage, but one that is intertwined with all the other phases of grief.* You begin to acknowledge the need for the positive aspects of your life again *because* you also continue to acknowledge, when present, your very real grief.

You may realize you are embracing acceptance through the little things of life. This morning I found myself singing along with a song on my car radio...and feeling good about it. This was a small step of pleasure that I know was not possible for me a year ago.

You may feel more inclined to participate in social activities, and recognize you are doing so not because friends and family are urging you to, but because it feels right. You find more things are funny and your laughter more genuine. You feel a tinge of motivation to return to a creative activity, or feel like starting a new one. Your physical environment may seem more beautiful at times now than you recall, even though it is the same place you have been for years. Your consciousness is awakening, little by little, to the reality of your new solitary life, to the possibility of renewal and to the deeper understanding of the mysteries of life and loss and how they co-exist for you.

~~~~~

RENEWAL PRACTICE ONE: RELEASING YOUR GRIEF

When I returned to Maine months after Marty's death, I ran into a well-meaning acquaintance who offered her condolences and then proceeded to advise me about what I needed to do to heal, to feel better. Her advice was to return to

the world, be with other people, go right back to my
volunteering work in the community. Despite my
omnipresent sorrow and limited ability at that
point to communicate that pain, I immediately
answered, "No, thank you, that is not what I need.
What I need right now is to be alone, to cry and
talk to the trees, to be in the comfort of nature and
the place, the home by the sea, that Marty loved. I
am not ready for more people."

You are the only one who really truly
knows what you need after the incomparable
loss you have suffered. I was lucky in that
moment to be conscious enough to know
what I needed and what I could not handle.
But the struggle to know how to handle my
grief in the long term has been an extended
learning process.

Although time itself diminishes grief's
intensity, it does not eliminate the pain you
may experience years or even decades after
your spouse's death. Time alone is inadequate
to heal your heart. What you do with that
time, how you recognize, respect and release

your grief is the essential foundation to begin to engage more fully in life, rebuild your strength, rise above the suffering, empower your elder wisdom and face the challenges of ageing alone.

Grief that is not released may linger within, generating not only more emotional pain, but physical illness. We have probably all known or met someone who is perpetually angry or sad or easily guilt-ridden. The powerful energy that is grief must go somewhere — or be stuck in one place. As an elder widow you are already more vulnerable physically and psychologically than almost anyone who has suffered severe loss at an earlier age. When you fail to release your grief you run the real risk of increasing all the suffering you already know. *But when you do release your grief, you open a space within and create a psycho-spiritual cleansing process that begins your renewal.*

Any of the following techniques can be used whenever you feel saddened, angry, guilty, fearful or shocked by the loss or memory of the loss of your husband. Or you might use any one of them or a combination as simply part of your continuous healing process. You will know best, after trying each one, which technique is the most helpful at any given time. I offer these to you only as a guided start, for as you try any one of them you may find that your own inner voice guides you to an adaptation or even a new possibility. What is most important is that you always acknowledge what you feel to yourself. You have the right to all of the feelings triggered by your loss. Sometimes, simply asking yourself, *"What am I feeling right now?"* begins the release process.

1. Vent Your Feelings. Speak with an open heart to a trusted friend, family member, minister, counselor, coach—anyone you know who can be a compassionate, non-judgmental listener. If no one is available, talk to your dog, your cat, the trees outside, a photo of your spouse or even yourself in the mirror. The act of speaking your emotional pain out

loud can be a mighty and effective healing force.

2. Take Time Alone. Solitude allows you to become more in touch with your pain and how it affects you. Meditate or simply be still in a quiet space indoors or outdoors, wherever you experience a positive, calming energy. Close your eyes, breathe in and out deeply and slowly and focus on thoughts and images of peace and tranquility. If needed, use a guided meditation CD or simply peaceful music as a background to your solitude. This is a particularly easy but useful technique when you are troubled by feelings of anger, resentment or guilt connected to your husband's passing.

3. Journal Your Feelings. Keep a notebook nearby in your home, by your bedside, in your car. As emotions suddenly or unexpectedly surface about your husband, your life together, or even of his dying, jot down the feelings in a bit of detail or simply name them. This is an ongoing life tool that

can help you acknowledge the reality of your pain and ease its release.

4. Try Out Energetic Body Work. Acupuncture, body massage, cranial sacral therapy, or Reiki are all therapies that work on the premise that grief, like any strong emotion, is stored in the body, in muscles, nerves, and tissues. Of course, this direction is one that challenges the financial limitation of many elderly widows, since most alternative therapies are not covered by insurance. If this is your concern, as it was mine, do not allow it to define your exploration of these very helpful techniques. I was able to bargain services with a few practitioners who were sensitive and sympathetic to my plight. Also, Reiki is often offered free of charge in group settings in many communities.

5. Consider How to Use Your Voice to Vent Your Grief. You may feel like singing, even if it is a sad song, or chanting or screaming. You may want to talk to your husband's photo or what you perceive to be his spirit. As you vocalize in any way that

suits you, you may find that raw emotion is triggered and suddenly begin weeping or feeling very angry. This is all part of the normal grief release process. Our feelings cannot be planned, but we can give them safe opportunities to emerge.

I have used all of these techniques at varying times and frequencies. For me, solitude in nature has afforded the strongest, albeit the most painful, release. Painful because my aloneness in itself brought additional suffering. And strongest because without the distraction of others, there was only my crying, which brought relief. Alternative energy therapies have given me the gentlest, sweetest comfort as release often occurs as part of a long-term process. So I have needed to remember that release techniques are not necessarily about making things easier in the moment or having shock-type therapy to release the pain immediately, but about coming to terms with and honoring my innermost grief.

There are no short cuts to releasing the depth of grief you feel. However, the strength you gain by moving into its release is part of your renewal, part of the process of opening to the light that awaits at the end of the cave of your despair. *Let us remember that we are the elders of our time, women who have the resilience, courage, experience, understanding and compassion gained through a lifetime of caring, giving, loving and sharing.* This, then, is what generates our wisdom to guide our lives ahead and those who come after us.

The healthy, normal healing of grief means understanding that grief in itself is powerful. As an elder widow confronting a new lifetime of possible challenges, releasing that power also restores it to you in a revitalization of who you are. You can use that power to move forward towards greater serenity and physical, mental and spiritual well-being.

CHAPTER THREE
OH, THE YEARNING!

The afternoon of my husband's death I was emotionally exhausted and taking a much needed nap to escape the harsh truth of my devastating loss. I was lying on the sofa, alone in my short-term rental home where my husband had only visited twice since he had become a full-time nursing-home resident for nine months. In the middle of sleep I felt a presence, the sense that someone else was in the room. I awoke and "saw" or "knew" Marty standing near to me in the living room. He was dressed in what used to be his favorite shirt and pants. He was whole, healthy and robust-looking and he was also silent. I felt a calming energy of deep loving comfort from him and a feeling that he was there for me. I fell back asleep, much more relaxed, and slept better than I had in the entire last three years of his physical deterioration.

I realize there may be "logical" explanations for my experience. I also know it was real for me and has been true in varied ways for countless others who have lost a dear one. My husband came to me when I needed him the most. I believe he still does so, although not since that day in the same way, no matter how much I wish he would. I miss him and mourn him every day, and I also understand more and more that although he is not here as I wish him to be, he is nevertheless a guiding, helpful presence in my life.

All the aspects of your husband's physical presence, now gone, can create a soul ache that feels impossible to address and does not end. You have spent most likely many years or decades together and suddenly it is all gone; his voice, his touch, his hugs, his laughter, his unique way of walking, talking, gesturing or joking can easily cause on-the-spot outbreaks of grief. I missed my husband's physical presence so much that for weeks I wore his jacket indoors, the only one that had not been washed and still had his smell. I held him close in that jacket and cried and cried for his love. I continually yearned for a renewed contact such as I had known on the afternoon of his death.

The reality of his being gone on the physical plane can truly be unbearable, and yet even as you know it to be an unattainable goal, you long to connect with him still. His physical self is absent. You have memories, you have a lifetime together of creating children, a home, memorable experiences and events—and yet it is not enough when you are spending your days and nights alone, a woman facing her own ageing and often feeling lost and disconnected on so many planes. You are dealing with so many new aspects of elder years alone, from financial to health issues, and the person who was there for you who knew just what to say and how to help, or was simply available to you by holding your hand, has vanished. You find yourself fearful, frustrated, anxious and craving over and over his caring company.

It is natural to desire to talk to your husband when his presence is sorely missing at any time of personal need. For an elder widow who is learning and struggling to live alone after sharing life's challenges for so long, the talking may feel weird and silly, for there is no visible response. You may feel that others would think you strange — the stereotypical old, lonely woman who is experiencing mental decline. You may judge yourself for believing in the moment that your husband cannot really hear you or help you, and then become even more upset and frustrated. And yet your heart yearns for his loving understanding and listening, his physical being. And it is often this yearning for him that feeds your grief and keeps you stuck.

However, there is simply no proof that he is not present with you at every moment that you need him. You have lived long enough that now is a time of life when what you need and believe is what really matters, not proving it to others.

I believe the soothing connection we crave is possible, if we open our hearts, spirits and minds to a new level of connection, in possibly a different form or manner. Some ways may depend on your belief and acceptance of post-death experience; others only require the time and space to honor all he has been to you. Whichever way you choose may be a means of calming reassurance that, despite his leaving the physical plane, he is still very much present in your life, perhaps even available to help you through this unique passage as an elder widow.

~~~~~

RENEWAL PRACTICE TWO: RE-CONNECTING TO YOUR SPOUSE

When I returned to our home in Maine after Marty died, I was overwhelmed with tasks of house maintenance, especially since his memorial was to be held in our home within a few short weeks and family was arriving from 4 states. It seemed there were just too many things I did not know how to do or had never done, from the simple checking of batteries in the flashlights to dealing with leaks in the bathroom. How very much I had depended on his mechanical know-how and skills, and how inadequate I felt on a daily basis without him! One morning I simply could not stand it anymore *when confronted with an automatic generator that was making strange noises and giving out unreadable notices. I knew I could not afford the $200 or so it would cost to have a repair guy come to my house, a distance of over 100 miles. I also knew I needed that generator operational since a power outage, not uncommon, could ruin the memorial service.*

I sat down and cried. "Marty, I cannot do this. I need your help. I do not know what to do. Please help me!" I soon calmed down from the crying and then had a sudden, unexpected, urgent thought to go outside and check a part of the generator that I had already checked three times. When I did so I noticed for the first time that the "off" button was not fully released. I released it and the generator returned immediately to its normal "ready to run" status.

I cannot prove that my husband is still with me. However, on every occasion that I have asked for his help, his ideas, his assistance for my daily battles with this new life alone, Marty has been there for me. I have had thoughts I never imagined having alone as solutions to problems. I hear in my mind his voice with calming, loving affirmation. People have shown up for me in situations when I needed assistance and had asked Marty to send me someone. Regardless of what spiritual beliefs I may hold about life after death, I realize *no-one, no-one* can say with any certainty what the post-death realm is like or what the person who has passed on may be capable of. I still may doubt myself at times, thinking it is my imagination, but the truth is I am surviving in realms of life that once kept me frightened and intimidated. What has made the difference time and time again is my connection to my husband in ways that are beyond the bounds of ordinary physicality. I ask for his help and ideas and answers appear. That is not a coincidence to me. It is reaching into a different dimension and finding hope and renewal.

You have lost your husband's physical presence, but not his spirit, not his love, not his words, and I believe, not your connection to him. Whatever ways you choose to re-connect with your husband you will find greater consolation for your grief and loss simply through the process of activating a new kind of connection.

1. Use His Photo as a Vehicle of Connection: You may already be doing this automatically in your need to share your daily problems and experiences with the person who shared them with you for so long. Merely make this a more routine occurrence by speaking directly to his photo on a daily basis. Ask him for solutions or new ideas for your challenges. Tell him about a new happening with a grandchild or family friend. Talk to him about your feelings of being alone, of dealing with the stresses of ageing. Reach out with love and hope and faith, and you may be surprised at what transpires.

For me this practice at times has turned into an automatic writing experience. When I look at Marty's photo I then write down, after a short meditative pause, a question I have for him. Every single time I do so, I am given an answer to my question that comes to me in that moment to write down. On other occasions, as in my experience with the generator, by asking the question out loud I come to have unexpected thoughts and ideas that address my questions. Most of the time they come to me immediately, but sometimes it takes as much as a few days. My husband never let me down when I needed him most in life and it seems he continues to be the same for me after death.

You may need to experiment with differing ways of reaching out for this connection. Try different times of day or when you are in different emotional states. Not everyone will have the same kind of connection with their departed spouse as we all have different personalities in life as well as differing types of connections with one another. Marty was a quiet man most of the time and loved silence and peace. His preferred time of day was the evening. I now find night-time is the best time to reach out to him and I have felt his presence more likely at that time of day. His answering thoughts directed to me are always as gentle and kind as he was. You may discover that your communication with your husband is best on a golf course if that was his favorite place, or at sunset if that was when he was the most relaxed. You will possibly find the connection in this manner evolving as I did or you may be consoled simply by the practice of speaking from the heart to your beloved.

2. Create Rituals to Honor Him. For his or your birthday, for your wedding anniversary or during holiday time when you are missing his presence the most, consider making up an easy ritual to honor him and what he means to you. If you are visiting his grave site or the place where his ashes are scattered, write and speak a loving prayer of your own to remember him. Light a candle near a favorite indoor space of his and place objects around it that symbolized something dear to him. Think about making this a permanent space and adding objects each special day, making it an altar of remembrance where you hold his

memory and love. You will, certainly with practice, as you reach out to his spirit, remember more clearly what he was like and feel his presence more definitely in your everyday life.

3. Ask for an External Sign of Connection. Asking your spouse outright for any proof of his post-life existence requires a leap of faith for many and may be difficult even for those who believe in life after death. I have been blessed by visits from many loved ones who passed, including cherished pets, after death in a dream visitation. Yet, while believing in post-life contact, I have waited and waited for Marty to visit me in dreamtime, and this has not yet happened. Nevertheless, he has been in my life and in my surroundings in so many other ways and forms. Once I acknowledge that his presence might not be what I expect, new contacts abound, from telepathic communication to animal visits and electrical energy.

In Your Life After Their Death, renowned medium Karen Noe tells us that our departed loved ones are eager to communicate with us, and that we can facilitate the process through our understanding of their mode of communication and being open to asking for and receiving the mode of communication that our loved ones choose.

The September after Marty died, seven months after his death, when my loneliness was extreme at times, and when I had begun to despair that Marty would ever come to me in the form I expected, I realized I needed to let go of my preconceived idea of how he might connect with me. One morning during my prayer time, the idea came to me to ask him to appear to me as a bird that I had never seen before in my home environs. Two days later, as I was driving down my 750-foot driveway, suddenly out of the woods appeared a very large white turkey. It was beautiful, with black wing tips and resplendent feathers. I was intrigued, as I had never seen a white turkey before and certainly not one near my home. However, I simply thought of it as a rare sighting until two friends visited me later that day and reported that they, too, had seen the turkey and wondered at its size and color. The next day while I was out on a walk, the same bird came out of the woods and actually started following me, trotting at full speed behind me. I became a bit alarmed. I had once raised chickens and the rooster, large and fierce, often tried to attack me. I had lost all memory of my request to Marty, and in that moment was only concerned for my physical safety.

I walked faster and so did the turkey. It was also vocalizing turkey speak — funny as that sounds, it is the only way to describe its continuous gobbling while running after me. I walked fast enough that I lost it as I left my driveway area and walked a mile or so down my secluded road.

But when I returned to my driveway, there stood the turkey as if waiting for me. Like a bolt of lightening, the recollection of my request to Marty returned to me. I stopped in my tracks and spoke to the bird, asking for proof of his being there for me. "Marty, if this is you and you are here to help me, please come around closer to the house to tell me you are with me. For now, please let me pass."

The bird walked back into the woods and I returned safely home. And at that point the whole experience was surreal. I had trouble believing that my request to Marty was being heard, let alone answered.

Early the next morning I was awakened by my cat meowing and chirping on the window seat near my bed. I guessed she was possibly watching a chipmunk or a chickadee on the ground outside, one story below, as she often did. Yet her chirping was urgent and louder than usual. I went over to the window and there, below the window of the bedroom Marty and I had shared for many years, was the white turkey, looking up at the window and once again "speaking."

I wept and thanked Marty for his loving appearance to me.

There is considerable literature describing post-life communication stories, and animal forms are one of the most common signs. In these contacts, the animals that appear always behave in manners that are not usual for that creature. If you have an experience like that, allow yourself to take it in and remember that you are not alone, that all is possible when we love and are deeply connected to another — whether in this earthly dimension or beyond.

4. Create a Way to Honor Who He Was in the World. You lived perhaps a lifetime together, and in all likelihood no one knew more about your spouse's interests, passions and sense of purpose. Whether your husband loved golf, art, operatic music, soccer matches, reading, hiking, politics, gardening, or simply what he had done for his daily work at one time, you most likely were the recipient of his stories, the sounding board for his ideas and frustrations, maybe even a participant in his favorite activity with him. *How would he best like his interests and passions to be remembered and supported in the world?* How can you honor him through his involvement in a world beyond your marriage, an involvement that characterized who he was as the man you loved?

Marty was an exhibit black and white photographer of the Maine Coast, an activity that never rose to the level of financially supporting him, but one that he pursued with devoted time, energy and heartfelt passion. I knew that, for him, the greatest reward of his work in photography was that others appreciated it enough to hang his unique visionary art in their homes or offices.

As the recipient of all the work he left behind that he had abandoned, having lost the will to promote it any longer, I took most of it and donated it to places where it would be visibly loved and remembered. It was a mammoth project going through hundreds of old prints, sorting, cleaning and cataloging what he had left me. And it was truly painful. Every single beautiful photo brought back a memory of his talent, his artistic sensitivity and his creative zeal, all aspects of who he was that I adored and missed. But once the photos were donated to grateful community organizations and galleries that he would have approved of, I felt such relief. I felt that he was closer to me than before, smiling at me for acknowledging who he had been and paying tribute to what he had accomplished.

CHAPTER FOUR
HOW ALONE IS ALONE?

What was your husband to you? What do you miss the most about him? How did he support you and your life together during the many years you shared?

Any spouse can be a helpmate, a comfort during countless occasions in life, providing companionship, loving acceptance of who you are, a cheerleader for your attempts to meet challenges, a confidant and best friend. But when you are living in this inevitable ageing time of life, with your own mortality facing you sometimes daily, the feeling of being totally alone, the absence of an understanding long-term mate, is overwhelming. Especially if you are an elder woman who is still grieving while facing financial struggles, health issues, social isolation, diminished energy and extreme loneliness. As an elder widow who lived almost a half century with the same partner, I realize I am continually having to recreate whole new systems of support for myself. The old systems I counted on for 49 years are no longer viable.

While family and friends may offer assistance and sympathy, there remains a powerful need for ongoing, unfailing supportive understanding. After decades of sharing history, stories, and even a common vocabulary with your husband, you ask yourself, who else knows all of this? Yes, a few others may know bits and pieces, but the long-term, live-in support you received consistently from that one individual can never be duplicated. Your unique life situation, more than ever, thrusts you into a sense of indescribable confusion and often a sense of helplessness when life problems arise or simply when you are missing a comforting touch.

Yes, I miss my husband every day for so many reasons and in so many situations, but the clearest feeling of loss often comes when I realize there is no one around anymore who can share with me with all the certain memories of our long life as a couple. Too many times, when I see or hear something that reminds me of an event or experience we had together, I start to turn around and look for Marty so I can ask him to fill in details of what I have forgotten. *"Marty, who was that man, what was his name, who sold us our first house?" "Honey, do you remember when we went to the Bahamas as a family? How did we arrange that then when we had no money?" "Oh, look at this photo of you and our daughter at 3. Do you recall how you and she would sit for hours watching the small creatures on the beach? What were you two talking about then?"*

The support we often crave from another lies in the small details of life, the feeling that we are being heard, understood, cared about on a daily basis. A healthy marriage offers the unconditional support of a mate who is present for your concerns and celebrates your victories while building a life of memories with you. Since Marty passed, so many well-meaning people have said to me, "Well, at least you have your memories." Yes, but I have memories that I do not talk about with anyone, because Marty is not here to help me feel their power by remembering them with me. It is possible that for the elder widow, already plagued by disconnection from the world, memories not shared with a living spouse may only serve to increase her loneliness.

Memories may only reinforce the feeling that there is no longer anyone in your life that truly knows who you are.

In creating support for myself I have come to the torturous knowing that the nature of some kinds of support will never be the same for me. There will never be another Marty for me. There will never be another person who knew me so well, who loved me in the way he did, who could anticipate my reactions in any given situation, affirm my memories, hold my hand without my asking because he knew I needed it, and understand my joys and sorrows without ever needing to speak a word to express that understanding. My marriage gave me the single most critical element of unconditional love:

understanding. That is a gift of many decades of loving and living together, and it can never be duplicated.

At the same time, I have also been learning *how to* survive without the ever-present support Marty's loving presence and complimentary life skills provided me. I no longer have readily accessible the emotional support I may crave, and neither do I have the support he gave me by being the household fixer-upper, the car-problem diagnostician, the financial planner and investor, the daily dishwasher and cooking assistant. When our spouses are there for us, essentially 24/7, our lives become a shared partnership in innumerable life arenas. And just as we begin facing the hardships of diminished physical strength, vitality and energy, just when we most need a helpmate, an understanding companion and cheerleader for our courage in enduring the trials of ageing, our partner is gone. As a woman alone at 65 and beyond it is frightening to wake up each morning and not know what new situation will come your way that will require you to develop new strength, skills, resources or courage, sometimes daily or on the spot.

When I was preparing my home for Marty's memorial three months after his passing, I had to deal with the fact that the house needed some major work. The entire outside needed re-staining, the extensive landscaping needed weeding and upgrading and there were numerous small outside jobs like caulking windows and doors that Marty had always attended to. I could easily see the problems, but had no idea how to do what was needed or the skills to handle them all. The money wasn't there to hire someone else to do everything. Marty and I had always handled all house upkeep on our own, having built 4 houses together, a couple of them totally by ourselves, from the ground up. But I had depended on him as the owner-contractor, for his abilities were present in the building, mine only in design and ideas and as his assistant. Now I had to find new solutions if I was to make my home and surroundings presentable again.

And I had to move outside my comfort zone to do so.

My personal comfort zone had been as a wife of 47 years working jointly with her husband. Now I had to rely on others — neighbors and friends — to fill in the gap. It was hard to be dependent on the kindness of others even when they offered to help. Even when I knew they were offering in the spirit of true caring. Especially when I really wished I could say, no thank you, I can figure this out alone.

And finally, I not only accepted help, but also began to ask for it. I figured out ways to show my appreciation, from well-cooked dinners to giving away Marty's tools. And I learned to accept help from those who wanted nothing in return.

To find support in maintaining my home at a critical time, I had to let go. I had to let go of pride and fear of vulnerability, of feeling the pathetic widow or old incapable woman. I had to surrender to this inevitable awareness: I was now an older woman alone who desperately needed the help and support of others who had never figured into my life this way before. It was humbling, and still is.

Yet it is also a critical piece of movement from the denial stage of my grief to acceptance of what is.

To find support now as an elder widow usually means to accept the reality that there is no longer anyone immediately available to help or assist in times of problems and challenges. It means planning for new ways to adapt to being alone, and knowing where to turn for help—whether for car repair, household repairs or a ride to the eye doctor for an eye exam that prohibits driving. It means knowing who to call when the grief and loneliness overwhelm and an attentive caring heart or simple companionship is all you yearn for. It means acceptance of the fact that live-in dependable, spontaneous support is no longer an option.

As elder widows we frequently live with many large and small fears and anxieties.

"What if's" rule.

What if I become seriously ill or disabled, how will I cope? What if I need help getting to a doctor or recovering from a surgery? What if I have unexpected expenses not covered by my health insurance or home insurance and my limited income does not provide? What if the roof leaks? What if the furnace gives out? What if I fall on the ice or down the stairs and no one knows I am alone here? What if I lose my car keys when I am out at the market and there is no one I can call who is available to come get me? What if my home is broken into while I'm here alone?

Where and how do I get the help I need is the question inherent in all the fears and anxieties an elder widow is prone to. Since over 70 % of all elder widows live alone, sometimes in declining health, many far from any family, and since there is a 40% loss of Social Security income after the death of a spouse, the intense fears of economic and physical helplessness are all well founded.

And the social isolation of elder widowhood only reinforces these fears.

Now, as an elder widow, it is easy to feel the misfit. Many of your friends may still be married and cannot grasp or do not wish to grasp the omnipresent loneliness you experience. (Since most married women after 65 will become widows, it is understandable that facing that reality early through someone else's experience may not be a comfortable option.) Adult children and grandchildren may live at a distance or have full, busy lives that do not include time for visits, so being part of a family once more does not feel feasible. You meet younger people who often have no true idea of the loss you have endured and are enduring and you find it difficult to relate. You are subject to the onset of sudden grief-and-loss feelings that can make you hesitant to be part of social or community groups when you cannot identify with the normal positive emotions of others. Far too often you find yourself the subject of an anti-ageing culture that already diminishes the worth of older individuals, and now you no longer have a companion to offset that sense of invisibility.

You may feel old, afraid, alone, sad, and even, sometimes, worthless.

It is a time of life when support for all you are going through is the most critical and yet seems the most unlikely.

And yet I can tell you from my own extreme isolation that no matter how alone you may feel, support can be there. It is not always easy to find. It is not always obvious. It requires from you an openness and desire to feel better and live again. You are being asked to dig down to the deepest level, to surrender your pride, false beliefs or a sense of understandable victimhood in order to ask for and accept the path forward in a new way. *It becomes imperative for you to seek and use all the support you can find to move into a fuller, less anxiety-ridden life.*

It is time to recognize that you now require enormous support because you have undergone and are still facing enormous change. You have lost the most present and consistent long-term support system of your life with the passing of your husband. And now it is time to claim connection to others as part of the pathway to the wisdom and renewal that, as an elder widow, you have earned.

~~~~~

RENEWAL PRACTICE THREE
CREATING INNER AND OUTER SUPPORT

OUTER SUPPORT: This is the support that comes from outside yourself, from individuals, groups, or community resources, to help you address challenges of living problems such as dealing with house or car maintenance or finding a ride to a doctor's appointment or psycho-social-spiritual issues like working through your stages of grief. It may also be non-human support in your environment such as the unconditional love of a pet companion when you are feeling sad or alone.

1. Find an Elder Widow Group. There are thousands of these groups. They exist in many cities and large towns and can be found through community centers, churches and simple networking. However, in smaller

geographic areas, if you are willing to reach out, your need can still be filled. You may have to be creative and take initiative to find or establish a group like this, a group which can uphold you in your transition process from grieving widow to wise and re-birthed elder woman.

Living in an isolated remote rural area with a tiny population after my husband died, I had no access to community groups focused on elder widows. So a year after Marty's death I contacted a local community education center to offer a support class on elder widowhood. Only a few women showed up, but the group was invaluable not just to the participants, but especially to me as the leader of the group. I found that most of my feelings as an elder widow were mirrored and understood at a level that no one else could imitate. The ever-present sense of aloneness seemed to vanish for me and each woman every time we met.

There also developed a social connection for two of the women in finding a new understanding friend to share activities with, a friend who needed no explanation for the often inexplicable waves of grief that could overcome without warning, a friend who was willing to join in adventures as part of the immersion into a new way of life. This is the value of what has become known as "elder women tribes"–widows traveling together, dining out, taking hikes, becoming caretakers for one another or sharing homes and apartments in the model of the well known TV show "Golden Girls." This phenomenon, described in Ken Dychtwald's book *Age Power*, is a way of garnering comprehensive support around a shared sense of loss, a loss that only another elder widow can truly understand.

For some widows who have been fortunate enough to be the beneficiaries of a large insurance policy or accumulated wealth, these elder widow groups provide opportunities for luxurious get-aways together or shared visits to expensive spas. However, since two fifths of widows become part of a poverty cycle within five years of losing their husbands, an elder woman's tribe might serve to provide the security of supportive friendship and possible sharing of resources and ideas on economic survival while preserving one's independence. Being part of a group who intrinsically knows what you are experiencing allows you to be comforted as you find your way into this new life stage.

2. Seek Out the Wise Friend or Counselor. By the time you have survived even a few months of widowhood you may realize that others, close friends or even family, who had wept or sympathized with you have moved on and are no longer easily attuned to your loss. They no longer ask how you are doing in your bereavement or how you are surviving in your life alone. And yet the yearning for your spouse's comfort and understanding remains, as well as your struggle to adjust to your new life without his companionship. You may feel that even a trained counselor will expect you to be taking steps back into

the world when all you really want to do is talk about your former life with your husband.

Six months after Marty passed, a close friend who had not been able to attend the memorial visited from California. Doris was not only compassionate but wise in her loving time with me. On a long walk together, she asked me to tell her in detail all the myriad aspects of Marty's long descent through his years of suffering into death. It was an extraordinarily therapeutic experience to be able to relate all that I recalled about those years as well as my lingering feelings of deep loss, guilt, depression and fear. Doris knew not to judge or advise or interrupt with her own stories, but to simply listen – the most important valuable skill of a wise friend or counselor. The self-imposed silence about Marty that I had been keeping because I didn't want to burden my family or friends was lifted. The emotional release for me at that time was the greatest of all possible gifts.

There is a feeling after we lose our dearly loved spouse that he is not really gone, and *that feeling* is not the same as denial. For he is present in all our memories of many years, in our daily habits, in our self-talk, in the familiarity of our surroundings, in our thoughts. And so it feels like a betrayal at times to deny his existence. There were many occasions after Marty died when a friend would be relating a story about her husband and I just wanted to share a related one about Marty, but I felt left out, as if I were bringing up an unhappy topic inappropriately. Yet a part of me was screaming: *"They are treating him as if he is dead! He will never be dead to me. He will always be part of me and who I am."*

It took some courage to break out of my limiting anxiety of being inappropriate, but I now more often share my Marty stories with friends and family when the stories are connected to the topic at hand. On a couple occasions I have even told friends that if they wanted to help me they could ask about Marty's habits or personality traits when they were revealing the same about their living husbands. This has alleviated a lot of the social discomfort for me and especially has helped me feel more supported and understood.

If a wise friend or counselor does not appear on her own in your life, you may have to ask for what you need. And you are likely to discover that your friend or even your counselor is relieved to know that so simple a thing as clear attentive listening or asking questions about your husband's life can bring you such peaceful comfort.

3. Seek Out Financial Counsel. The uncertainty you experience as a new elder widow is far too often magnified by fears of financial security. If your husband was the financial manager, these are now anxious times as you struggle to understand the reality of now managing alone your very limited or even abundantly large estate. You may not even know how to balance a checkbook or know where certain funds or securities are located. Even if you were a full

partner with your husband in financial arrangements, you likely feel the frightening loneliness of now making all the decisions on your own. You have no idea how many years are left to you and no idea what to expect in terms of medical and health expenses, not to mention continued cost-of-living increases on often set income amounts. Life ahead of you feels so uncertain on so many levels that the idea of taking care of money and figuring out how to have enough to live on can be paralyzing.

Immediately following Marty's death I felt deluged by financial arrangements: not just payment for leftover medical and cremation expenses, but all the changes required in credit cards, bank cards, savings accounts, mortgage and investment accounts. I found myself often in tears trying to make the needed phone calls and having to explain over and over the same request to have names changed, funds moved into my name, or even to establish a new account with a credit card company that had known us both for 30 years. The impersonal bureaucracy of it all plus the host of totally unfamiliar financial terms became a nightmare for me as I was struggling to figure out if I even had enough to live on.

I was saved by a caring financial advisor who had become the investment manager of our retirement funds shortly before Marty became ill. She was sure of what to do and how to do it and totally understood the terms of all the financial gobbledygook. Most importantly she was sympathetic to my grief and fears. She took on irritating bureaucrats, advised me clearly of what to do and even what to ask and continued to monitor my situation as I made plans to become more independent in managing my financial future. Her support — kind, concrete, expert and reliable — was an immeasurable aid in helping me release the terror of doing it all on my own.

Your estate following your husband's death might be very simple or quite complex, very small or quite large, but what matters is that you are relieved of making long-term financial decisions by yourself at a time when you are emotionally vulnerable and afraid. A trusted family member may be able to help with details, or perhaps a loving friend or a known, reputable banker can recommend someone who can be there at least in the short-term to help create a viable financial future for you. You are in a process of becoming stronger and more self-supporting as you create a renewed life. Ask for and allow yourself the essential practical support of someone who can help you with your financial needs while respecting your time of life.

4. Distract Yourself. It may seem odd to think of distraction at this time in your life, especially when I have been emphasizing coming to terms with your new life situation, but healthy distraction can play a supportive role in doing exactly that. When you are feeling beleaguered by new responsibilities, by old memories, by fringes of depression or intense loneliness, seeing a delightful comedic movie or a silly TV show, listening to some uplifting music, playing catch with your dog,

or taking part in a fun group activity can give you a much needed pause to recuperate energy, inner strength and a more positive mood.

The trials of elder widowhood can feel, and in reality often are, too much to take in. In the first months of the first year, especially, it seems impossible to catch your breath from the siege of endless new responsibilities and fears. Going outside your daily routine of readjustment through a light, distracting activity can be the much needed break you need. This, too, is often the area where friends and family are usually more eager to be available. While many may feel uncomfortable talking with you about your emotional life, they are likely to be more than willing to accompany you to a movie, a church supper, a musical or sporting event. And you may return to the reality of your widowhood refreshed, realizing the beginning twinges of knowing it is possible to now enjoy some parts of life without the company of your beloved.

For me, living in a small community isolated from many possible distractions, the idea of distraction took on unique meaning. I had no Internet access at my home, my closest geographic friends were few, my family all lived in other states, the nearest movie theater was over 100 miles away and my funds were extremely limited, prohibiting any real travel outside my town. But one day when I was feeling particularly lonely, I put on a CD of sixties music that Marty had not enjoyed, but that I did. I played it at the highest volume, knowing that no one else was around to be annoyed by it, and after a few minutes found myself dancing and singing along. I even went out on my waterfront deck and sang to the seals! It was fun and uplifting and gave me permission to feel the first sense of true freedom from my ongoing emotional pain. And in my heart I knew Marty would have approved, even if he did not like the music.

INNER SUPPORT: This is the support that comes from within you to take charge of your life in new fear-reducing ways, now that your loved one is no longer physically present to provide that support. It is the support that is especially critical for the elder widow who is isolated from family, no longer has a work setting to provide meaning, or has not been active previously in any community based groups. Most importantly it is the support that is always there for you whatever your situation, once you tap into its limitless base of inner power and your lifetime of acquired wisdom. This inner support system is based on your awareness of what works for you. It is key to moving into a healthier phase of greater acceptance and renewal of a meaningful purposeful life.

1. Practice Positive Consistent Self-Care. Immediately following your spouse's death, you most likely find it almost impossible to care for yourself well. Sleeping may be troubled, eating not appealing, and exercise almost un-thinkable. As you release more and more of your grief and move toward a greater integration of your new life, self-care might

feel somewhat less challenging, but still not always a priority.

Yet it is imperative as an elder widow, who is already at the highest level on the stress scale, that you commit to maintaining your health and even improving it every single day. Your risk factors for serious illness are high. You may feel like that doesn't matter, that you are too alone to care. Cooking feels too much a chore alone and eating alone too sad. You are too tired out by all your new responsibilities to exercise. But every excuse and reason takes you down a path to possible physical decline.

This must now be your innermost question: Do I want to survive and truly live the life I have left?

For the truth is that self-negligence of your physical body is self-destruction.

Self-care may be the place you have to push yourself the most. This can be truly the most critical self-care time of your life. It's a time to create the physical building blocks of your healthy whole self through abundant sleep, nutritious food and regular physical movement. This lays the foundation to help you claim, envision and discover the life that you are transforming and re-creating: the life of elder, wiser woman, a woman who has endured and is still growing, living and learning.

After almost 5 decades of cooking for my husband and sharing thousands of meals together, it was devastating to cook and eat alone. Marty loved food, loved my cooking, and meals with him were always, for me, a time of feeling valued and appreciated. Dinnertime was also a time of talking about our daily experiences. I found cooking by myself to be not only lonely but confusing. I had trouble figuring out how much to cook or even how much to buy in groceries for just one person. Right after he died I was fortunate enough to live near my daughter, so we often shared a few meals each week. And I avoided a lot of cooking by buying nutritious and reasonably priced take-out at a local health food co-op. Cooking, a creative activity I had always loved, simply lost its attraction for me.

When I returned to Maine, and my daughter and family were now thousands of miles away and the nearest healthy take-out 45 miles from my home, I found myself not caring to cook at all. "What is the point anyway?" I found myself thinking. Life was just too hard, the loneliness too intense.

But somehow the habit of taking excellent care of my physical body kicked in and I made a conscious decision to eat well again. Perhaps it was for no other reason than to not become ill and be a burden to my daughter, who had already borne so much responsibility during her father's long physical deterioration.

Now I had to act on that decision, still feeling no desire to cook or eat alone. I took baby steps, preparing small meals and sandwiches at first and then making larger meals I could freeze and defrost over several days. I learned to make myself choices of frozen meals so as to not become bored with just one.

The shopping and cooking, with time, became easier, more gratifying, especially when I was able to invite friends or neighbors over to share a dinner or lunch. What was significantly harder and still remains a challenge is the eating alone. I have shifted my dinner place so I no longer sit opposite an empty chair, or when possible, I eat outside, or read a book or even watch TV to change the environment for myself. Listening to music or the radio often helps, as does saying a prayer before eating and being grateful for what I have before me. Yet the bottom-line reality is that I know for the rest of my life most of my meals will be alone. I can embrace the quiet and solitude, which I often do well, or I can feel sad and alone which, at times, are feelings that still rule.

Either way, my acceptance of my life first lies in my acceptance of what I feel and then letting it go. And each week, each month, becomes filled with more grace and strength as I empower myself to be as healthy as I can be.

Once you have decided to live your life more healthfully again, it is still too often difficult to take on the tasks of self-care all alone. Those who have offered to help you in your widowed life can now be called upon as exercise buddies or occasional food shopping or meal companions. Or invite into your life a loving pet friend if you do not already have one. I have frequently found that my cat is a more consistent devoted companion at meal-time than anyone else!

Now is also a good opportunity, if you are not yet doing so, to explore some positive body energy work, which will not only help with alleviating your grief, but increase your incentive for overall improved self-care. Regular energy work can improve your sleep patterns, and consistent restorative sleep is key to positive mood enhancement, which makes it possible to actually enjoy your solitude when necessary.

Attending to self-care is a hallmark for the emerging woman you are, the beginning of a woman in her elder years who values her life enough to save it and live it wisely to its fullest.

2. Practice Self-Acceptance and Self-Love. You have gone through and are still experiencing a period in your life when guilt and regret may often rule. You may have

repetitive memories of your husband's illness, his manner of death or your relationship, which cause you to blame yourself. Although self-blame and guilt are normal parts of the grieving process, even after the greatest intensity of grief is behind you, these feelings frequently linger and disrupt your path forward.

How do you free yourself from so many self-sabotaging thoughts which hinder your freedom and potential to claim your life?

Here is the place for beginning the fine art of self-forgiveness. *Forgive yourself for what you did not do, what you could not do and what you wish you had done.* Consider the possibility that even had you done all you know now, your husband would still have died. We cannot truly know the future nor can we know with any certainty what a different past would have been created now. There is a spiritual principal that teaches that forgiveness is liberation: it gives us the freedom to let go of self-harming thoughts and beliefs. It opens up a place in our hearts for more love and compassion, for ourselves and for others.

Imagine your husband still with you and tell him what you need forgiven. Imagine what he might say, how he might respond. Recall the love you felt from him and the answer will be clear.

The power of forgiveness lies in the honesty we bring to it.

I still find I am repeatedly plagued, now more than 2 years later, by the pain of knowing I could not save Marty's life. And the truth emerges that the self-blame can keep me stuck as a victim. I am transforming into an elder woman who is living and surviving and even thriving, but it is heart-wrenching to remember I am doing so alone. *Can I truly claim my own life? How dare I live on without him?*

Love is an eternal force, a sacred uplifting feeling of freedom. Holding on to self-blame is an ego construct that blinds us to the truth of who we are and who we are becoming and contaminates our love. Who are you now that you are a widow who still loves her husband, but seeks a more complete life? And what would your husband's loving wish for you be?

Self-forgiveness is not easy and there is no clear formula. It begins with allowing yourself to be human, to make mistakes and at times to have poor judgments. Whatever you did or did not do regarding your husband is all wrapped up in hindsight. It looks easy now and yet the time and circumstances are no longer the same.

Although I continue to recall the decisions I made regarding Marty's health issues, I know today those decisions would not be the same. My knowledge base is different, my fears are no longer present and so overwhelming. I am more clear-minded. I realize I did the best I could knowing what I knew and given the choices before me. So when at times I still grieve those choices I must remind myself that Marty loved me too much to blame me, and I need to do the same.

As a spiritual principal it is also helpful for me to allow Marty to have had his own path. Perhaps his suffering and his death were his journey and mine was to love him and comfort him the best I could while he was with me. And now my path is to release him and any self-blame that pollutes my renewal and his memory.

Consider ending each day with a thought of forgiving yourself for any action or word you feel guilty about, and sleep will be sounder. When you begin to truly forgive yourself, you open the gateway to self-love, to accepting your new life as inclusive of and deserving of greater joy.

3. Shift The Energy that Keeps You Stuck. So often you may feel that nothing works, that you are stuck in a cave of despair, self-pity and hopelessness, especially during the earliest months of your mourning. As an elder widow, life may simply feel like too great a trial. When depression, sadness or anger seem to be a prevalent mood of your day, think of it

as an opportunity to try a shift in your internal energy.

First recognize and honor your feelings, and then move your psyche and body into a new space. Sometimes just taking a brief, fast walk outdoors can do that. Or if you are more aerobic-exercise oriented, a long bike ride, a swim at a local pool or workout at a gym can help ignite those positive endorphins that create a more positive mood. If sufficient sleep has been a problem, a quick afternoon nap can be refreshing enough to motivate a fresh, rested outlook on life. I have found that the negative ions in water make a difference for me: when I am feeling so low that it feels hard to go on with my day, an extra shower seems to lift my mood. If loneliness is holding you in its negative grips and no friends are easily available for company, perhaps a visit to a local store or library can at least give you the human contact that will switch your frame of mind. It only matters that you discover for yourself the ways and possibilities that empower you to become unstuck, to realize once again that a fuller life yet awaits you.

4. Engage in Regular Spiritual Practices. Beginning or continuing with regular spiritual practices can be the single most effective inner support you give yourself. This will connect you to a greater sense of being, of wholeness, and depends on nothing more than your own intention. As someone who has been involved in varied spiritual activities for over 40 years, I know personally that they have been the most transforming and healing element during this unprecedented period of isolation and loss in my life. I cannot even imagine having moved into any level of true acceptance without the support of my spiritual practices.

It is not necessary to join a group or take a class or belong to a church. Any of the practices listed below can be done on your own, in your own time and according to your own spiritual orientation.

~ **MEDITATION** This age-old spiritual technique, when practiced daily, brings calmness of mind, body and spirit. In 15 or 20 minutes a day you can access your connection to higher mind, experience greater relaxation and clarity, calm anxiety and restlessness, become more in sync with your authentic being and lessen your grief and fears. Through focus on the breath or a mantra, you begin to tune out the clamoring voices of the self-defeating ego mind and the outside world and tune into the stillness that enhances serenity and overall well-being.

When just beginning a meditation practice, it is sometimes helpful to use "guided meditation" or visualization CDs. However, it is silence that allows your inner voice to be heard and guides you through the new challenges in your life. To be truly in touch with your own unique inner source, true meditative quiet is the most productive practice.

~ **PRAYER** No matter how you define God or higher consciousness, prayer will bring you closer to knowing and reaching greater spiritual solace. The power of prayer lies not in asking for outcomes or desires fulfilled, but in believing in them. Consider prayer as a vision, a thought, an idea that aligns you with higher purpose. Prayer for guidance, understanding, strength, wisdom or knowingness is the place to begin your prayer practice. A single prayer such as " I believe and trust all is well and in divine order" or " I am protected and loved by God" can bring a greater focus on your connection to the divine and a trust in a higher order that dissipates inner fear and diminishes outer struggle.

~ **GRATITUDE** This may be the most difficult of spiritual practices given the indescribable loss you have suffered. It often feels as is if there is nothing to be grateful for. Nevertheless, the act and expression of being grateful for all you have in your life increases your awareness of your abundance and allows the energy of abundance to become more drawn to you. Begin simply with spoken or written words of thanksgiving addressed to a higher consciousness, for your loved ones, those dear ones who are still with you, who have been there to comfort and help. Think of and be in thanksgiving for all those who have helped you along this journey, even the kind strangers who have lent a hand or wished you well. Perhaps you are able to be grateful for positive aspects of your health and physical well-being, the companionship of a pet, the inspiration of nature, the solace of times of peace. Soon you will come to realize all that you have almost every minute of your day...from the simple ability to draw breath to the beauty of a tree or flower you pass on your way home. Making yourself conscious of your enormous abundance by the daily practice of gratitude is one of the easiest ways to increase the vibration of joy. And in the process of this practice you will find that you become blessed with more and more to be grateful for.

~ **NATURE** Sit by a tree, stroll through the park, meditate on the shore, study or read in a garden. **Only be, simply be**, in a place of greenery, natural growth and forms and sounds. Here is the balm of Divine Oneness with all creation, the connection of earth energy with the essence of your spirit. Nature rests, restores, inspires, heals and blesses all those who respect, seek and immerse themselves in its gentle, life-giving and divine power. Take a moment to be enfolded in nature each day and you will experience a difference in your life.

When I returned to Maine after my husband's death, I entered a life of unbelievable isolation. My home, which had once been our summer home but was now the only home I had, is located on the tip of a peninsula, surrounded by wild forest, over 2 miles from a paved road and a 14 minute drive from a tiny town. No neighbors are visible or easy to find, and my friends there, although loving and caring, live a quiet life and are all married. I no longer had much work of my own, having had to give it up for my husband's care and our frequent moves connected to that care. And the work I did have was all by phone with no in-person contact. At first, arriving in summer, I had more opportunity to see other people, to connect with summer visitors or be involved in a get-together at someone's home or at my own. Then the Maine winter came on and I had to face the tough reality of increased isolation and the fear of living in an extremely remote place by myself for the first time as a woman alone in her seventies. Internet was not possible at the house and contact with the outside world at all was extremely limited. Friends were all engaged with husbands in the rigors of normal survival tasks like stacking wood, getting ready for the onset of the winter's rages. Days would go by without the presence or sound of another human being. Snowstorms would whirl, howling 60-70 mph winds surrounded the house, ice covered my exits and driveways, and leaving the house was often unthinkable. I grieved greatly not only for Marty's presence and company, but for his help in surviving and enduring it all.

My spiritual practices literally saved my life.

I prayed daily for strength to persevere, to not fall into an abyss of despair and loneliness. This degree of isolation coming on the heels of my loss made me vulnerable to frequent thoughts of leaving the planet. And yet, every time it became too intense and I turned to prayer, within a short *period someone would call offering support, or even more miraculously, I would feel, even though still alone, a sense of no longer <u>being</u> alone.*

My 45-year meditation practice calmed my fears as well. I began to believe that no matter what, everything would work out. I would survive. That motivated me to learn how to deal better with the problematic effects of living where I was and taking care of my home alone — from knowing when to sweep snow off the deck before it became frozen or how to store salt for use on icy walkways to who to call in a true emergency.

The time spent in spiritual practices is time that continually helps me define my inner core, my belief in something greater than my circumstances and emotional pain. I can access that source anywhere or anytime and know that support is there, that despite lingering grief or loneliness, I will continue on.

The probability of spiritual practices helping the transition from grieving to acceptance is borne out by a study done in Canada in the year 2000 with elder widows and widowers. The findings suggest that several specific aspects of personal inner meaning in life, including spirituality and religiosity, tend to alleviate depression and anxiety following spousal loss, improve coping and well-being and provide hope and comfort.

What is especially outstanding is that widows, much more clearly than widowers, indicated the positive benefits of religious and spiritual support.

As an elder widow you may well be struggling to belong again to your community or to society at large. A religious group or church may not always fit into your belief system or you may not feel like being part of a group at times. A consistent spiritual practice that can be done in your own time and space may be the route for you, as it was for me, to renewed adjustment and inner security and growth during a truly unstable time of life.

When you acknowledge the inner connection to a Source greater than yourself, you tap into the power of a revitalized belief in your own purpose. You have been left

behind, the surviving spouse, and you might
wonder, what is the point? Consider that your
life is a gift, a blessing still to be treasured. As
you sense the serenity of meditation, the calm
wonder of nature, or feel a divine relief
during prayer, you begin again to claim your
own intrinsic value which not only heals your
heart and expands your consciousness, but
benefits others in your world.

CHAPTER FIVE
ENTERING THE NEW PATHWAY

As a woman who has experienced a lifetime of joys as well as sorrows and who is now facing years or decades alone without her life's closest partner, I find I am constantly challenged to find new meaning in my life. I believe that meaning will be birthed and will bloom not only from the lifetime of experience I carry within, but also from the seeds I have been planting at this moment in my time of elder widowhood.

The wisdom of your life is now in play in every aspect of your new stage of life. This time can be an opportunity to become someone you have always wanted to be or someone you have already been and did not acknowledge enough. For I have discovered the truth that lies within the pain, sorrow, agony, fear and anxiety: This time of great loss is also, intrinsically, a time of enormous growth and self-evolution.

The question, now as you move in and out of acceptance and imagine the years that lie ahead, is: Now that you are no longer a wife, no longer a helpmate to your beloved, who are you as a woman in your later years?

I spent a lifetime being with Marty, 47 years of marriage plus 2 years of dating, and throughout that time I worked in the outside world. I was never a stay-at-home wife or mother. I was well educated and considered myself well-rounded, not identifying myself by my role as a wife.

But losing him, losing that vital connection to his love, to the life we shared as a couple and as a family, losing the reality of daily companionship and support, no longer being able to give to him in myriad ways every day of our life together — it woke me up. I was, in fact, a wife, inside and out. I had an identity that I had never fully recognized as key to my sense of inner meaning and purpose. The love I showed him every day, the meals I cooked for him, the encouragement I gave him in his challenges, the admiration I showed him for his accomplishments, the listening I offered to his struggles and the home I decorated to provide comfort and peace for us both, all gave my life significance. I was a wife who enjoyed her role and yet never fully considered what my life would be like without it.

The years ahead may be many and without the sense of completion that being a wife can bring. Yet you have gone through and are still experiencing the fire of pain and loss and assuredly a feeling of needing purpose. And in the depth of all you have endured, there lies opportunity. If you dare to truly listen to your inner voice and open yourself to renewed identity, direction and service, you can transform your loss as an elder widow into a time of transition from victim to survivor, from wounded to healer, from sorrow to clarity of purpose. All that you have experienced creates an opening to manifest a life of elder years embodying decades of wisdom, inner strength and resilience.

The challenge of being older, widowed or not, is that ageing is discounted in our society. Grey hairs and failing physical strength are all too often looked upon as a disability rather than as signs of many years of valuable experience and learnings. As we enter this period of life as women alone, that sense of invisibility is heightened by the absence of a life partner who made us feel, through his love and support, that we mattered. Even when adult children or grandchildren seek our advice and knowing, geographic distance from them can make those opportunities too infrequent to create a sense of ongoing purpose.

So now is the time to move from the past of caregiving and supporting a spouse to a time of caregiving and supporting one's self. Now is the time to become who you still may be, a woman with strength and inner power, a model for the next generation. It's a time to share and pass on what you have learned. The sacred way to transform grief and enter into a renewed time of life is through the path of earned wisdom.

It is now over 2 years since I became a statistic, an elder widow largely ignored by society at large. At this age I seem to meet more women who are passing through this doorway that I have only recently entered. And my compassion for them knows no bounds. Although I have always been known as an empathic person, finely tuned by my counseling and coaching work, this period of loss in my life has magnified my vision and understanding so that I immediately feel what a new widow in advancing years is experiencing. My heart is touched and my soul yearns to help. This book is my foremost attempt to reach a larger group, to offer any wisdom that I have gained to help other elder widows find their own renewal. And in doing so I am aware that I also create and embrace a renewed purpose for my own later years.

As you move down the pathway from wife to widow to the unknown, there is an opening that awaits, an entrance to embracing and using fully that unique gift of inner knowing that defined elder women for centuries as the wisdom keepers. This is, for me, the pathway that promises to yield greater awareness of my direction, my movement into the last years of my life with a fuller honoring of who I am now that I am no longer a wife. This unique time in my life is the last opportunity to give and grow and evolve to my fullest capacity. A time to grow my inner self as well as my outer experience. A time to embrace joy once again, but now as an elder widow. A time to share my expanded self that has endured the heartbreak and isolation of devastating loss and who is now surviving and at times even thriving. A time to live my spiritual self, to come to each day with greater compassion, understanding, patience, generosity, kindness and acceptance—all aspects of my being that have awakened more completely during this time of grief and loss. All qualities that may now also lead *you* forward into your renewed life.

RENEWAL PRACTICE FOUR:
TRANSFORMING YOUR GRIEF

*As my husband was slowly dying I often felt a
great part of me was dying with him. My ability to
feel joy, my ability to be optimistic and to find a
greater vision in the midst of ongoing suffering,
my ability to have faith in the future, to believe
that all would ever resolve itself in some bearable
way — all of the positive aspects of my inner life
seemed to be dying. Hopelessness overcame me at
times not only while he was dying, but then also
even more frequently after his passing. I lost my
way from being a woman of accomplishment and
success, empowered from within, to being a
woman victim without direction, purpose or
identity, alone and lost in the outer world. Yet,
little by little, I have been emerging into a new
light-filled life. I can, with conscious thought and
awareness, see and appreciate the gifts I have been
given during this heart-wrenching time. I
appreciate all that I have learned and am more
attuned than ever to my inner voice. This level of
consciousness brings inspiration for ideas to
manifest and belief that they will be worthwhile.*

As I have mastered more and more of the once dreaded tasks of daily living from car and house maintenance to financial management, all formerly my husband's domain, I have gained new self-assurance and confidence. As I have released my innermost deep grief in my own way and time, I have felt a renewed interest in socializing and community activities, which has brought me greater connection and support in the outer world. When I reconnect to Marty in another dimension I can feel his ongoing presence and that comfort continues to uphold me, knowing he is supporting me in my path ahead. And as I daily carry on with my spiritual practices I experience the increased faith and inner fortitude to discover who I am now.

I know now, from my very deepest knowing, that I will never return to the life I once had. And even as I still often grieve for that life, I am also *beginning* to see that what lies ahead could be, for me, the most powerful years of my life.

1. Acknowledge Your New Skills and Growth. Throughout this difficult elder

widow's walk you have been gaining fresh insight not only into your own emotional life, but also into the life of your everyday reality. Due to your highly changed circumstances you have had to learn new skills, new approaches to daily life, new responsibilities and new knowledge. You have had to take on much of what was unthinkable before your husband's death, and yet you have survived and perhaps in some arenas, even thrived — all at an older and more often fragile time in your life. Take the time to review a different perspective of your individual growth. Ask yourself, what is the positive side of my new life? What can I do now that I never did before? How am I stronger, more capable, more self-reliant? What have I learned about being alone? You have faced fears and trials that you might never have imagined. As you gain new awareness of the resilience and learning you have achieved, you lay the foundation to understanding who you are now and what is your place in the world at this stage of life.

This past week has been a week of restoring my home for the advent of summer. The ravages of winter have taken their toll on the structure and grounds, and it has been a daunting task to consider many much-needed improvements. Reliable handy men for help are scarce here and my own budget extremely limited. Finally, after trying for weeks to secure some help, I decided to try some repairs on my own in areas that were always Marty's domain. After grabbing tools that I am not at all comfortable with and balancing with some trepidation on a small ladder, I removed some protective boards on the screening of the screened-in porch. I then went on to repair the broken half of the screen door. Lying sideways on the cold porch floor and figuring out a way to hold tools and use the repair glue at the same time would have made me laugh if I had not wanted to cry so badly. I thought "I hate this — this is not the life I want or enjoy and I am not any good at this!" But finishing the tasks and looking over my handiwork, simple as it was, made me feel a sense of mild pride. After Marty died I had no idea even how to begin anything like this. I was so mechanically and technically impaired that changing batteries in my TV remote was enough to make me feel helpless. I have come a long way in at least being willing to learn more, undertake more, in previously untouchable areas for me and especially believing more in my power to do so at this older age. It has been a difficult, uphill learning curve, but I know I am becoming stronger as a result.

Your burgeoning and often difficult new responsibilities may not be fun, but they do enable you to see yourself in a new way if you are willing to open that door. You might discover that you have a hidden talent you never before realized, even if that talent lies in finding or coaxing someone else to help you! You are a survivor, not just in mere living, but in making your life work by dealing with everyday tasks. As a survivor you are possibly emboldened to learn more, to increase your skill set or to feel the confidence of someone who believes in herself.

Undoubtedly, you have also grown and evolved in an emotional realm. The security you once knew when you had a loving supportive companion at your side is gone. Financial security may be a lost promise. Reliable outside support may still elude you. The future feels uncertain. The question I often ask myself when security in my world feels missing and I fall into anxiety or fear is: *Where does my security reside within me?* Where, my sisters, are you finding the strength to prevail, grow and become stronger? What aspect of your inner self has developed that now connects you to your ability to keep learning how to survive and claim a fuller life even past 65?

However, the daily and emotional learnings of living are not even close to what you may have learned about dying.

Marty's dying and death undid me on so many levels that it may take the rest of my own life to see it all from a wider perspective. But one thing I know clearly: his passing affirmed that death is not final and not to be feared. The moment of his death I felt his essence move, I felt the energy of his spirit and I felt his peace immediately after. I have felt his presence time and time again since his body left this plane. I have known him to be with me countless times when I needed his support and love. This is truly his greatest gift to me. For as I approach and live into the final decades of my life, I am able to do so knowing there is more beyond. I am able to grasp more fully the concept of preparing for my own demise by making my last years more meaningful and by being more present with my own spiritual life.

As you reflect upon the loss of your own dear life's partner, there is within all the pain, suffering and grief a possibility of life renewal borne from your own learning and understanding of death itself. Your journey forward and how you thrive is connected to how you see death and what it has taught you about how to live.

2. Activate Your Intuition. As an elder widow you have gained innumerable new aspects of life wisdom borne of harsh and

painful reality. As an elder woman your past surely includes decades of dealing with crisis, nurturing children, helping friends, caring for your spouse or ageing parents, taking care of a home and contributing to your community. Through all these situational challenges and caretaking you have gained strength and ageless experience that can be shared to motivate and inspire others who come after you. This is the intelligence of your outer life that has grown from more expansive thought, emotional stretching and increased knowledge, the training ground from life itself.

The wisdom gained from long life experience also teaches, if you heed its call, that life needs to focus not on an ego-centered, outer-world acceptance, but on inner self-acceptance. Who are you? What is your own self-knowing? How do you grow your inner gifts and inner self?

Through all the trials of becoming an elder widow you have surely gained more courage and more compassion, as well as a new sense of tenderness and even possibly a greater pleasure in the increased solitude of your life. This is all part of an emotional level of maturity that allows you to judge yourself and others with greater love and generosity.

And I invite you to consider intuition as your door opener, the key to an extended world of wisdom that continues to expand as you practice it, activate it and act upon it. As you move forward into greater renewal-seeking a more purposeful life, the wisdom of your inner life, your inner intelligence, can guide and transform your life. Your higher consciousness, your inner guidance system, is best able to help you know which turns in the path ahead to pursue, who or what can help you, which new adventures or possibilities you need to explore. As critical as all your knowledge and insight gleaned from life challenges are, it is this inner guidance that truly generates a powerful transformation of loss to a wisdom that ushers in a new life of meaning.

During the most intense early months of my grief I often heard in my head the words "elder widow." These were words that had particular meaning to me, not simply because I was a recent widow, but because I had for many years believed we need to look at older persons as "elders," not "elderly." "Elders" traditionally are the revered wisdom keepers of a tribe or community, whereas the term "elderly" too often conjures up visions of disabled, frail and commonly-believed-to-be useless older adults. At the time, my grief was too overbearing to pay these repetitive words "elder widow" much attention.

Nonetheless, the words kept tracking in my mind as if they had a will of their own. Their pattern brought on the insistent urge to take some sort of action. I did not know what that action could be until I happened to come upon a flier for a community education center where I had once taught classes. In my new overwhelmed life I had forgotten about that center, but immediately a light clicked on in my consciousness. So a year after Marty's passing, when my pain was fairly raw, I felt the clear strong need to offer a class on the topic of elder widowhood at that center.

Although attendance was low, it became the catalyst for me to begin writing this journal and guide.

We never truly know where intuition will lead us, but trusting it can be a journey of enlightened and unexpected surprises.

Up till that time, in that first year after Marty's death, I had been unable to even imagine what my path forward could be. I was many times lost in a sea of depression and loneliness as well as fear and doubt about daily living, finances, health concerns and extreme isolation brought on by my geographic location. I had given up most of my independent work during his illness and no longer lived in an area where I could again cultivate new clients. The idea of re-creating my life felt, at times, like a fantasy.

I was also a woman who had taught innumerable classes and led countless groups on cultivating intuition. I had a lifetime of being a highly intuitive woman who had used that knowing to lead and guide my life and help others do the same through classes, public speaking and life coaching. And yet I thought I could no longer tap into that knowing so effortlessly as I had always done. **For the truth is that intuition is blocked by profound grief and powerful emotions of any kind.** The reality is that my intuitive self had always been present, but at first I could not hear its insistent and subtle calls. Now through my opening, finally, to those calls, I have come to believe more profoundly that my life still has purpose, not simply because I am still here, but because my intuition keeps guiding me to new directions.

It is easy to avail yourself of the innumerable books on developing intuition. And at the end of this guide I have listed a few possibilities I have discovered to best access your intuitive knowing. Through my classes and groups I have learned that each of us accesses our intuitive knowing in differing ways. However, the universal key is the ability to stay open to reactivate that voice which is inherent in your inner self. As an elder woman you already know, through a long lifetime of experiences, that there is often another way to go beyond simple emotional reactions to life's most painful challenges. Your maturity gives you a vital perspective, but it is your intuition that can provide you with the higher-level guideposts as you step into your expanded time of life as an elder widow.

3. Recognize and Embrace Your New Freedom. It may certainly feel like a sacrilege to point out that having lost the heart center of your world, you might have more freedom. Yet the reality is that despite the pain and grief and loneliness, you are more likely freer as a widow in many areas of your life than you have been in years or decades. This is especially true, as it was for me, if you were your husband's caregiver during an intense or prolonged illness and decline. And it is also true for some of the daily aspects of life that you shared and in which you perhaps needed more time or space or opportunity to be you.

If you had trouble sleeping with a restless or snoring spouse, you can now appreciate the luxury of a bed all to yourself. If you became weary of constantly preparing meals for two, you can now relax with a quick easy dinner salad for one. If you had often craved more time to yourself for hobbies, friends, exercise, your own music, reading or just being in silence, now that time is yours to expand as you wish. You may even have more financial freedom due to increased income or simply the freedom to make your own individual choices about money. And yes, yes, I know, you likely also feel that you would, in a heartbeat, trade all of that new freedom for even 2 or 3 more hours spent with your beloved. I completely understand and identify with that feeling. And I also acknowledge that my husband is gone from this plane of existence. I did not choose for his death to occur. Acceptance of his death means to know at a deep level that he is not here, and what remains for me is the reality of my time now, what it is, what it is not and what it can be.

My husband and I were so close that even during just a day apart we would usually check in with each other several times by phone. It was always a comfort to hear his voice and be able to share my day and hear about his before we reached the end of that day. Our conversations were not necessarily in depth, but they could be lengthy and they could entail a reminder of some task I needed to fulfill for his needs or our life together. It always buoyed my spirits and gave me fresh energy to speak with him. I no longer have that daily support and connection, but I do have instead the time to pray, to sleep longer, to relax more, to take care of my own needs only. And at this later stage of life those activities are prized for they provide me with much appreciated self-care.

Time is precious as we age, for it no longer feels limitless. As time frees up for me in differing ways since Marty's passing, I know I have more choice about how to use it. I savor my quiet hours and believe they fill me with a sense of greater peace and calm.

My time in solitude, although excessive because of where I live, is, nevertheless, often a gift. My freedom to plan my own day without the constraints of anyone else's needs allows me to have less stressful days. I cannot say where I am headed as I continually heal and see the advantages of greater freedom, but I do feel as if I am on the brink of claiming a greater self, of leaving a legacy of my own lessons and growth to those who may also pass this way.

In older, pre-Christian times, pre-patriarchal times, elder women were leaders in communities, midwives, surgeons, spiritual leaders, health and child-care advisors, leaders of ceremonies, scribes, and caretakers of body, mind and soul for their community from birth to death. In those times, elder women were revered as fonts of wisdom and sought out for their skills and knowledge. Wrinkles meant the presence of a wise woman, someone who embodied maturity, understood the cycle of life, was strong, courageous, insightful and powerful. This woman, the grandmother of the tribe, was known as a Crone—a term that today is sadly associated more with being powerless, an old "hag," an embarrassment of senility.

In Goddesses in Older Women, author Jean Bolen describes the periods of horrific persecution of Crones for almost 2 centuries. As many as 8 million women were feared for their gifts, abilities, intellect and property (mostly widows), and were persecuted, tortured and killed. During this Women's Holocaust, women of Crone age were at the greatest risk. Women in those days learned to stay inside, to become invisible. It was too dangerous to be noticed or seen as a wise woman.

Ms. Bolen believes that as elder women we carry that fear of being seen in our DNA, a fear of burning at the stake if we listen to our inner truth.

But as elder widows who have endured so much, who have survived, it is now time to face our fear of being visible and become who we can still be.

It has been said that true personal power comes from knowing who we are and what is our place in the world. Now that you have been stripped of your role as a wife, as a partner, as a companion to your loved one, you enter a fresh dimension of seeing your power at an advanced age. The loss you have endured, the trials you have suffered, the growth you have experienced and the intuitive wisdom you have gained as an elder widow are the foundation blocks of that power. As you contemplate the remaining years of your life, the intrinsic questions that you may consider are deceptively simple: What is my purpose? What do I pass on? What do I want to create now in my world and in the world around me?

Every life is unique and each of us as an elder widow has known varying and difficult circumstances and challenges. But there are common threads of experience and feelings as we deal with the most life-changing loss of our later years. Patience, endurance, flexibility, openness, gratitude, trust, forgiveness, acceptance, surrender, kindness, resilience, courage, faith and fortitude are just a few of the life-enhancing qualities an elder widow must develop and cultivate in order to not just survive but thrive again. And these are all qualities that enable you to move into a deeper level of sensitivity not only to your own experience, but to all those who face pain, loss and intense transition. We are assaulted by severe loss at a highly vulnerable time of life, but we also come to it with a lifetime of learning how to surmount difficulty. We can then emerge from the cocoon of indescribable grief to a time of fresh expansion of our hearts built on a decades-old layer of inner strength.

As I write this, I know my truth is that I am growing stronger and feeling more centered in my life more of the time. I also know that there are still many periods when I feel the overwhelming loss and pain and fear that came upon me at the time of Marty's death. At those times I wonder if I can continue to claim my life again, if there is a future and purpose in my remaining years.

It is the core question for every elder widow: How do I move forward?

I believe we can move forward by giving from our hearts. Coming from the most wounded place in us, as we heal our own center, we can reach out to the need for healing around us. It is a time to love again. Time to love yourself fully and gratefully. Time to integrate the sense of peace, serenity, greater confidence and renewed strengths you have gained into the expansive power of being an elder woman. If there is a reason for all that transpires, there is surely a reason why you are not the one who left this plane first.

There is still more in your life to explore, to experience, to understand and to share. These are the later years of your life, but also the time, as acceptance grows and time for yourself increases, to shift the focus from sorrow about losing the life of your beloved to a greater presence in your own. After years of giving to another, of being there for him, the years of connecting to your own choices with a deliberate sense of freedom may now begin.

I know I will miss my husband and all we shared until I exit this earth. I also know his love for me is eternal and that his wish for me would always be that I continue to live fully, that I find joy, pleasure, love and, most especially, meaning in my life, no matter what my age.

And I am beginning to genuinely believe that is possible.

May the blessings of potential renewal find their way into your life and heart as well. May your journey as an elder widow blossom into a walk of love, peace, purpose and connection to all that serves you well.

SIMPLE HINTS FOR USING AND DEVELOPING INTUITION

1. Pay attention to inner "urges" on a daily basis.

What do you feel like doing when you first wake up in the morning? (not what you "should" do!)

Is there someone you just "feel" you need to talk to? (even if it seems illogical?)

Do you have an attraction to a particular new learning or skill?

(Even though you think you may be "too old" or untalented to try?)

Is there a duty or responsibility you have that you feel drawn to give up? (But you feel obligated or irresponsible if you do that? Is it time to let that go?)

2. Take small *action* steps in practicing your intuition.

Imagine actually doing what you would like to do first thing in the morning — and how would you do it?

Call the friend or family member you are thinking of — and just ask how he or she is.

Get some information about taking the new class or undertaking the new learning — explore the possibility and see how that "feels."

3. Write down any vivid dreams, gut feelings, everyday images or mental sounds that come to you.

Put the list aside and then forget about it — after a couple days or weeks, look at it again. Does any of it make more sense?

4. Practice some *absolute* quiet each and every day. <u>Essential!!</u>

No TV, no phones, no music, no radio. Start with 5 minutes. In the quiet, unplugged. Simply ask your intuition to guide you or help with a specific question in your life.

5. Keep the idea of intuition in your conscious mind

Connect with accepting open-minded friends or family and talk about any times your intuition has worked for you. Tell stories, read articles on the internet about it...do whatever you can to acknowledge intuition consciously, and your unconscious mind will be triggered to access your intuition more.

REFERENCES/READINGS/INSPIRATION

WIDOWHOOD — THE DEMOGRAPHY OF WIDOWHOOD

http://medicine.jrank.org/pages/1840/Widowhood-demography-widowhood.html

ESTIMATED MEDIAN AGE OF MARRIAGE BY GENDER

https://www.thespruce.com/estimated-median-age-marriage-2303878

NUMBER, TIMING AND DURATION OF MARRIAGES

https://www.census.gov/prod/2011pubs/p70-125.pdf

THE FIVE STAGES OF GRIEF

http://grief.com/the-five-stages-of-grief

LIFE LESSONS: Elizabeth Kubler-Ross & David Kessler, 2000

BLESSINGS FROM THE OTHER SIDE: Sylvia Browne, 2002

GODDESSES IN OLDER WOMEN: Jean Shinonda Browne, 2014

YOUR LIFE AFTER THEIR DEATH, A MEDIUM'S GUIDE TO HEALING AFTER LOSS: Karen Noe, 2014

"ENJOYING LIFE AFTER DEATH" Joseph Shapiro, US News, Sept 11, 2000

"UNIQUE CONTRIBUTING OF KEY EXISTENTIAL FACTORS TO THE PREDICTION OF

PSYCHOLOGICAL WELL BEING OF OLDER ADULTS FOLLOWING SPOUSAL LOSS" PS Fry, PHD, The Gerontologist 1998

"LIVING WITH LOSS: A GUIDE FOR THE NEWLY WIDOWED" The Hartford Advance 50 Team

About the Author

LUCILLE ANN MELTZ, MA, MSED, owner of *"Touch the Soul"* Life Coaching, has helped hundreds of women deepen their spiritual awareness while accessing their intuitive knowing and inner wisdom through her inspiring classes, personal coaching, public speaking, hand analysis and guided meditations. Lucille lost her beloved husband of 47 years in March of 2015. She is now focusing her skills and experience on the largely unacknowledged life transition process of elder widows. Website: www.lucilleannmeltz.com

Prepared by LUCILLE ANN MELTZ "TOUCH THE SOUL" COACHING and HAND READING WWW.LTL-LIGHT.COM

www.lucilleannmeltz.com

Made in the USA
Middletown, DE
13 May 2019